Things That Happen...

Things That Happen Where There Aren't Any People

Poems by William Stafford

BOA Editions • Brockport New York • 1980

Grateful acknowledgment is made to the following publications in which many of these poems (or earlier versions of them) first appeared: *The Carleton Miscellany:* "The Dialectic of Mountains"; *Colorado Quarterly:* "By the Old Deer Trail"; *Crazy Horse:* "End of the Man Experiment"; *Dacotah Territory:* "Buffalo Skull"; *Ellipsis:* "A Place in the Woods"; *Field:* "Notice What This Poem Is Not Doing"; *The Genesis:* "Saint Augustine's Prayer"; *Inquiry:* "Remote But There"; *Mill Mountain Review:* "Crossing the Desert"; *Missouri Review:* "Hinge in the Wind"; *Northwest Review:* "A Hand in Water" (originally entitled "Dolphins Live Like Heroes Without Hands") and "Lines to Introduce Fragments from a Journal"; *Ontario Review:* "Nobody"; *Paumanok Rising:* "Wherever you Go on the Island"; *Quarterly West:* "Being Still" and "Dawn on the Warm Springs Reservation"; *Red Cedar Review:* "Learning Your Place" (originally entitled "Learned While Eating Popcorn at the Zoo"; *Seattle Review:* "A History of Tomorrow," "An Offering," "Any Old Time," and "The Early Ones"; *West Coast Review:* "A Treatise: Influence of Howls on the Frontier"; *Western Humanities Review:* "Things That Happen Where There Aren't Any People" and "Through the Junipers."

"Explanation" originally appeared in *The Hudson Review.*

"An Address to the Vacationers at Cape Lookout" originally appeared in *The New Yorker.*

"Answerers" was first published in *Contemporary American Poetry* (A. Poulin, Jr., editor, Houghton Mifflin Co.); "Things That Happen Where There Aren't Any People" and "Through the Junipers" were also previously published in *Contemporary American Poetry.*

Photograph © 1980 by Ed Reed

Publication of books by BOA Editions is made possible in part with the assistance of grants from: The Literature Program of the New York State Council on the Arts and the Literature Program of the National Endowment for the Arts.

Designed and printed at the Visual Studies Workshop
Typeset by City Newspaper
Binding by Gene Eckert, Inc.

Distributed by the Book Bus, Visual Studies Workshop, 31 Prince Street, Rochester, New York 14607

ISBN 0-918526-19-1 Cloth
        0-918526-20-5 Paper

First Edition: March, 1980

BOA Editions
Publisher: A. Poulin, Jr.
92 Park Avenue
Brockport, New York 14420

for: The Readers

*Did you think, all those times, I was
telling you only the words?*

CONTENTS

LINES TO INTRODUCE FRAGMENTS FROM A JOURNAL

Go, little book I never thought
would go: tell anyone who asks,
what truth you have. Remember that
your words were often quick
and meant for only friendly eyes —
the writer's own, which could forgive
as fast as pen could give
or friendly eyes could scan,
who said, "Come, any thought,
no matter how inane: try
your place in words and live
the way we all must learn to live —
any way we can."

NOTICE WHAT THIS POEM IS NOT DOING

The light along the hills in the morning
comes down slowly, naming the trees
white, then coasting the ground for stones to nominate.

Notice what this poem is not doing.

A house, a house, a barn, the old
quarry, where the river shrugs —
how much of this place is yours?

Notice what this poem is not doing.

Every person gone has taken a stone
to hold, and catch the sun. The carving
says, "Not here, but called away."

Notice what this poem is not doing.

The sun, the earth, the sky, all wait.
The crows and redbirds talk. The light
along the hills has come, has found you.

Notice what this poem has not done.

NOBODY

Quiet when I come home, you
leave every chair for me. You stand
by the window when I leave. Alone
in your dream I see you surrounded
by space — my dream too. The woods
you pass through stay the same, and I
love you for it. You came to my
birthday party, and I danced with you
all night after the candles burned out.

When I make mistakes, you always count
them, to be sure to credit my years
of service in your shadow. Now I grow to be
like you, and when trains go by the engineer
no longer answers to my wave. Recently
on a road I was traveling I looked far ahead
and saw you making the tracks in snow that
I was walking faster and faster to fill.
After I catch up and we travel on together
you will no longer need to make those tracks in the snow.

PLACES THAT WILL BE SAVED

Sacred for what's not yet done
a little rock rolls down
maybe by a road in the woods.
I watch for them — something is
a little strange, but nothing
happens but waiting, and then
this one event: I stand there, breathing.
Sometimes a touch of wind
passes ahead of time
when the rock rolls down.
The world and I go on.

Sometime the truth will come.

HINGE IN THE WIND

When they come by, I sing them away:
"Nobody home, nobody home,"
and the door stares back. I know they know.
But one by one the spiders teach them:
"Another place, it's another place."
They come by here, but here is gone —
not far, not near — it's everywhere.
It has no door.

Late snowflakes come drifting down,
alone and perfect, never the same.
They know I know: the spiders win.
There are no locks to hold the world.
Days leach past.
When the wind returns what will it say?
"Nobody home, nobody home."

ANSWERERS

There are songs too wide for sound. There are quiet
places where something stopped a long time
ago and the days began to open
their mouths toward nothing but the sky. We live
in place of the many who stir only
if we listen, only because the living
live and call out. I am ready
as all of us are who wake at night:
we become rooms for whatever almost
is. It speaks in us, trying. And even if
only by a note like this, we answer.

THE EARLY ONES

They kept it all level. And low. Even
little stones they swept away. They went on
for miles, a bend at a hill, then a bend
back. Around them birch forest mostly
or openings for lakes, and a few hidden lakes.

They carved on the rocks — these are what stay,
hardly worn at all if sheltered, some
broken and all of them gray, that distant
gray that clouds have, or storms that moan
at the coast. They carved and went away.

Level and low. And the carved things. And one
more thing: when you look around and listen,
the last thing is there. You hear it wait.
Because they were early and quiet, and because
of that last bend, and because of the gray —

There is something left. We'll find it some day.

END OF THE MAN EXPERIMENT

In The North a great wind lived.
Its mighty hand
scoured a kingdom out
and formed the last snowman.

What a strange carol he sang! —
himself blowing away,
lips, head, hands,
whimpering low, forlorn,

Till only the level wind
lived in that land,
the whole bowed world
one storm.

A PRETTY STONE

Some other year, if the sun,
if the moon, and the stars
come and if there are meadows
in the mountains for it to be night
or day or between, if no people
come, and a wind ruffles a lake —
inside this rock it will tick
once and be noon in your pocket
or wherever you carry it, even
if you just think (no matter how
slightly and with a shrug) of now,
of us, of the moon, of the stars, of
a lake where we picked up a stone.

EXPLANATION

They tell about a train
— nobody at all aboard —
that rolled for the bridge at midnight
and hit all the signals forward
where the Feather River canyon curved
lonesome between tall cliffs
guided by only the rain.

the man who told me — lied:
that empty caboose, those lights
nobody ever tended, or saw,
midnight looming, and the bridge,
and that deep canyon brimmed
with sound nobody heard —
there wasn't any such ride.

Emphatically, once and for all:
I've explained it a hundred times
walking at night with a friend —
how could anyone tell?
And it was a long time ago.
And it wasn't the truth when that train
wound through the dark in the rain.

LEARNING YOUR PLACE

They have other studies in their eyes
than anyone, the wolves that pace their bars,
priorities afar, and bonuses
no zoo-goer comprehends. "Invest a paw
and get a world," their shoulder says when they
turn. They own you once when you arrive,
then give you away for good: no elaborate
trial — a glance — you don't exist.

BY THE OLD DEER TRAIL

Into the forest under the bough,
and under the bough again,
feet by moss, lost — long lost —
a path veers toward our time,

Coming to meet what moss retrieves
after the deer are gone,
after the shy ones bunch their feet
and launch off into time.

Looking hard at the level moss,
the sun burns over the line
deer once made for the sun to burn
after their time, our time.

BUFFALO SKULL

All day devoted to earth
I lie where willows bow.
I confess all day,
face to the dirt and snow.

While willows run in storms,
bent low, never still,
and even the brave are afraid,
I dream: buffalo skull.

A TREATISE: INFLUENCE OF HOWLS
ON THE FRONTIER

Wolf howls alone devastated the West,
put a scare over the landscape, reared
snags against a faint moon; and people
with guns spraddled around, in falsetto
boasts giving their least cowardly boaster
the name hero;

Meanwhile flowing lightly around their
cozy night, wolves and their friends
the Indians pawed for scraps, offered each
other the jewels of their eyes, and
occasionally did a job of howling,
for fun.

A HAND IN WATER

They know headfirst those aeons when
Earth leaned on a bell and no one heard.
They swim a life within. Whatever light
there is, they search and search. They think
fingers; they stutter music.

Their mothers hold them; then the sea does.
Their love provides that swoop the birds have,
or wind or wave, as far and lonely. Then
all at once — as Mozart judged the world with
every note — their songs bring close the Hesperides.

We own the world now, out here, but leave them
a place. Moonlight — that coat our old generals
wear — may be their sky too. Put a hand
in water, there where time goes: the sea
acts out a requiem, that loom feeling, the years.

THROUGH THE JUNIPERS

In the afternoon I wander away through
the junipers. They scatter on low hills
that open and close around me.
If I go far enough, all sight or sound
of people ends. I sit and look endless miles
over waves of those hills.

And then between sentences later when anyone
asks me questions troubling to truth,
my answers wander away and look back.
There are these days, and there are these hills
nobody thinks about, even in summer.
And part of my life doesn't have any home.

WHEREVER YOU GO ON THE ISLAND

Built slowly from fog, led
among sticks and released forward
like a whispered word, a new day
realizes itself. Parts of a world
begin to know where they are. Anything
large enough to be noticed by dew
offers its mirror to light, nothing
too small to note, all ennobled
again, touched by some power above kings:

It's alive, the whole world is alive.
Breathe on its mirror again,
tease it along over the fern
lean with it toward the light.

THINGS THAT HAPPEN
WHERE THERE AREN'T ANY PEOPLE

It's cold on Lakeside Road
with no one traveling. At its turn
on the hill an old sign sags and
finally goes down. The traveler rain
walks back and forth over its victim
flat on the mud.

You don't have to have any people when
sunlight stands on the rocks or gloom
comes following the great dragged clouds
over a huddle of hills. Plenty of
things happen in deserted places, maybe
dust counting millions of its little worlds
or the slow arrival of deep dark.

And out there in the country a rock has been
waiting to be mentioned for thousands of years.
Every day its shadow leans, crouches,
then walks away eastward in one measured stride
exactly right for its way of being. To reach
for that rock we have the same reasons
that explorers always have for their journeys:
because it is far, because there aren't any people.

REMOTE BUT THERE

Mornings a shaft of light pauses to read
a stone beside a mountain path high
beyond the snow. I left it there one day,
climbing alone — for one who once was with me.

Dismissed after a glance, ignored by the dawn wind,
that shelter for my thoughts is my abiding friend:
no one now can find it, and only the sun reads
those erased years and the name I know.

A HISTORY OF TOMORROW

It is the stones, they say, that began
the quarrel, tripping the waves — imagine
that struggle for years. But water fought back
and broke up the stones, till mostly sand
was left. One thing the waves forgot:
after they break up the sand, smaller
and smaller, what is left? You can't
see it, but millions of little stones
drift back behind the waves and continue
their drift, with no clash, no sound —
they flow away. And for years now
at the bottom of the ocean those tiny children
of the stones have been huddling together, still,
heavy, into one big rock so deep
the waves don't know it, growing harder
and harder. The waves don't know it. They hit
the rocks that look big. The big one waits.

CROSSING THE DESERT

Little animals call
us, tiny feet whisper, and
a certain wide wing shadow
flickers down the gray wind,
flickers its menace over the
sage, and banks toward some equivalent —
a storm or mountain.

Pardon! Pardon! —
the ditch at night is a church
where eyes burn their candles
mile after silent mile
to meet whatever comes, whatever comes.

The next time this world is ours
we'll cry out from the ditch
to find our cousins there safe
offering us their paws and letting
the light we bring return from their eyes
to shine forth, part of our own.

WHAT IT IS

By luck, it finds where to flow.
Whatever stops it, it waits, then
turns to where nothing is. It
has forgotten as soon as there is
anything to forget. It likes everything
but never notices itself. When still,
it says the sky. There are whole camels
of proof inside it when it shies through
the desert. Seeing it, you know what passes, and
it is what you know.

DAWN ON THE WARM SPRINGS RESERVATION

Into its frost-white branches
a juniper draws the light,
a bowl of it, softly glowing, quiet.

Off through the fog all day
miles of these file away,
faint pearls of white.

And all spirits in the world so bide,
one for every thing:
a place, a tree, a rock. . . .

You can't give away, or buy,
or sell, or assign these hills —
they hold what they always held.

And it's the same all over the world —
any tree, any rock, any hill.

THE DIALECTIC OF THE MOUNTAINS

Descending at 60 the slow dream of the freeway
rounding Saddle Mountain by moonlight into the open,
our antenna stabs into the wide beam some station
    pours from the north:
eloquence rocks the car and we reel down through
    radio sound.

(Why did I learn so well to read? — loosing the phantom
mind for its endless lonely journeying through any page on
demand. "Goodby!" — it plunges, dives for life into the wave
it makes, and guided by everything offered it, it rests by
traveling. Authors bait it, sling it a joke, a talk, some soothing
wine — before the night is out it's gone again, through arctic
pages, the dialectic of the mountains.)

Tonight we read the Grecian Urn, resurrected Keats,
went into the solitude with him beyond the lines,
    melancholy
as frost forms on the pane, art everywhere. But up
    ahead
loomed guidance of the storm, our time,
we realized, on the way home: it takes a forever
    story to keep men warm.

(There is a net over the world. It is too fine to see. It does ex-
ist and make a difference. Things do not fall apart: even in
our time the only eloquence with real effect leads toward
piety.)

William Yeats, you orator, claiming the usual voice
    and then
shouting others down: it took us years to find
the real direction, after you. I admire your cape,
    boy, and odd corners of the thought
you swirl; but there are ghosts more real than
    your rough beast and all, in Sligo.

(Remember back in the hometown library: pursued by life
into the text and overtaken at every page, the mind hurrying
fearfully away, wading, then swimming, then drowning itself
in the ebb of the story, only to find a submarine world with a
book in it, snorkel of actual sound: someone shouting the text
of the day — Niagara — and the library shimmering back
toward air: "Closing time.")

Teachers live by trying, have to drive and go
    carefully past
the trumpet writers and beware the trumpet critics
    and go around
Saddle Mountain, and sometimes not even reply to
    challenges: not say anything
where there is nothing in the car for the wise to say,
    steering.

You need large eyes at night, throat for
    careful saying,
luck on the road, teaching State Extension
    Division Lit 109.

SAINT AUGUSTINE'S PRAYER

In the world of Augustine a part of God
everyplace in space (where in thirty minutes
five hundred billion years ago everything began)
began: a kind of hum.

Now everything is gone from where it was,
and how it was. Through galaxies rove
yesterdays, and in that roving the words like his
become their humming past:

Somewhere all he said rejoins a choir
streaming back to everyplace, a world
inhabited by a spark this great — so tiny
that it never moves, it goes so fast.

A PLACE IN THE WOODS

An early place — come near and look —
a place where light spreads its wide white hand;
from the air true shapes come — triangle,
circle, and a kind of line not yet found.

In your life you meet only flaws and whatever
drops into form by chance; and your hand
from chance reaches its way toward eternity,
performing its part of all your failures.

You get used to that, and most of the time
what comes is all right, but now your hand
here in this early place where the glow
of day passes a certain part of becoming —

Wants true dawn.

AN ADDRESS TO THE VACATIONERS AT CAPE LOOKOUT

The whole weight of the ocean smashes on rock;
the sun hounds the night; gulls ravel the edge.
Here it is better to allow for what happens, all of it —
the part assumed, the lie that keeps a rendezvous
with proof, the wickerwork that disguises the iron:
this place is too real for that blame
people pin on each other, for honor or dishonor.
    Have you noticed how uninvited
    anything pure is? Be brave — there is such a thing
    as helping history get on with its dirty work.

When the home folk tell you goodby
they shouldn't *bid* you goodby, that corrupted, wise way,
nor burden you with too great a gift; and I
wouldn't burden you, except with one great gift:
the cold, the world that spins in cold space —
to be able to walk away, not writhe in regret
or twist in the torture bush. After all,
there is such a thing as justice in friendship.
    All of the time, we know how uninvited
    anything pure is: here something big lifts us
    outside, scorns our bravery or fear.

What disregards people does people good.

ANY OLD TIME

Deep in the morning
all the trees behind one another
toward miles we don't know darken,
light barely touching their trunks while
their branches tangle the sky:

This is the still time that lasts,
caught and held. You hear birds
but their songs do not change,
while no change comes in that sky
as on other mornings that passed.

Forever drops into place.
The day will go by, saying no to both
dark and light: Now has found
what it looked for. Deep in the trees
light balances: our time.

Listen — you can hear day standing still
around all the miles wherever you are.

BEING STILL

Try it, being still in the mountains. They wait.
And where ferns have taken their kind of green
stillness you learn the slow steps of daylight.

Patience inside your life, a drop, a drop,
a drop: when the next moment comes you are
ready, no matter what's already done.

You look away — what you are unable
to do, you neglect. It has limits,
your life. Patience! Patience, my heart!

Beyond your hearing, a voice — it murmurs
and goes by: oh, where you are going
no one can lift the great silence of the sky.

AN OFFERING

Had you noticed — a shadow
that saves us when day stares
too hard? — inside our eyes
there's this shadow?

Sometimes the light stares
deep: the whole day glances home,
and shivering at the edge of something, you
know, you almost know.

But it's too great —
our failures help us recover
so we can stand our suffering.
I've noticed this.

And there is one shadow so great
we live inside it our whole life long.
And it is here right now.
These poems are for that shadow.

Winner of the National Book Award for Poetry in 1963, William Stafford's many other collections of poetry include:
Traveling Through the Dark (1963), *The Rescued Year* (1966), *Allegiances* (1970), *Someday, Maybe* (1973), *Stories That Could Be True: New and Collected Poems* (1977), and *Smoke's Way* (1978)

Things That Happen Where There Aren't Any People has been issued in a first edition of twelve hundred copies, of which six hundred are in paper and five hundred and fifty are in cloth. An additional fifty copies have been bound in quarter-cloth and French papers over boards by Gene Eckert; ten copies, numbered I-X, have been signed and include a poem in holograph by William Stafford; twenty-six copies have been lettered A-Z and signed by the poet; fourteen copies, numbered i-xiv and signed by the poet, have been retained for presentation purposes.